ECONOMIC ISSUES 9

Protecting Bank Deposits

Gillian G. Garcia

INTERNATIONAL MONETARY FUND
WASHINGTON, D.C.

ISBN: 1-55775-642-2
ISSN: 1020-5098

Published July 1997

To order IMF publications, please contact:

International Monetary Fund, Publication Services
700 19th Street, N.W., Washington, D.C. 20431, U.S.A.
Tel.: (202) 623-7430   Telefax: (202) 623-7201
E-mail: publications@imf.org
Internet: http://www.imf.org

Preface

The Economic Issues series aims to make available to a broad readership of nonspecialists some of the economic research being produced in the International Monetary Fund on topical issues. The raw material of the series is drawn mainly from IMF Working Papers, technical papers produced by Fund staff members and visiting scholars, as well as from policy-related research papers. This material is refined for the general readership by editing and partial redrafting.

The following paper draws on material originally contained in IMF Working Paper 96/83, "Deposit Insurance: Obtaining the Benefits and Avoiding the Pitfalls," by Gillian Garcia of the IMF's Monetary and Exchange Affairs Department. Alfred Imhoff prepared the present version. Readers interested in the original Working Paper may purchase a copy from IMF Publication Services ($7.00).

Protecting Bank Deposits

Over the past fifteen years, almost three fourths of the member countries of the International Monetary Fund have faced crises in their banking systems. These crises have led many countries to consider or to adopt deposit insurance to protect their financial systems from the impact of bank failures. Although the special importance of banks to a country's economy might seem to make the insurance of their deposits unquestionably worthwhile, the reality is not that simple. Banks are also businesses dedicated to making a profit in an uncertain market. As such they can take chances, overextend, and act imprudently. Banks are indispensable for the smooth running of an economy, but should society be unconditionally responsible for underwriting banking decisions, even those incautiously taken? Should folly be rewarded? Government authorities must tread a fine line between assuring the health of the banking system and encouraging recklessness on the part of individual banks by overprotecting deposits. Deposit insurance can therefore have pitfalls as well as benefits—ill-conceived deposit insurance schemes could seriously harm an economy.

Role of Banks

Banks are crucial to a country's economy; they serve as the center point of the exchange of money throughout the economy. They gather savings from small and large depositors, make loans, run the payments system, and coordinate financial transactions. In developing countries, they usually are the heart of the financial market and in industrial countries with complex financial markets they still have a role as primary providers of financial services.

It is difficult for the layman to know if a bank is financially solid. Banks may appear more solid than they really are. A bank that has loaned money to a borrower who is unable to repay may keep the bad loan on its balance sheet as long as possible, though the loan might never be paid back. Moreover, bank deposits are also somewhat precarious. A bank normally cannot refuse to accept deposits, but if, for whatever reason, its depositors lose confidence in the bank's soundness, they may withdraw their funds not only from that bank but also from other, perfectly sound banks.

In seeking profits, banks lend on the basis of their customers' deposits, but not all deposits can be lent out. A certain share must be held in reserve. Competing institutions providing financial services are in a different situation since they are usually not subject to reserve and prudential requirements. Firms selling equities do not promise fixed returns, and neither equities nor bonds are payable on demand, as are most bank deposits. Because of the pivotal role of banks and their vulnerability to unusual risks, there seem to be good reasons to protect deposits through an appropriate insurance scheme and, in this way, to protect both the bank and the banking system.

Opponents of deposit insurance, however, maintain that a deregulated financial system is best for a country's economy and that deposit insurance in the long run upsets the system by weakening incentives for bank managers, depositors, borrowers, economic policymakers, and political leaders to act efficiently. In theory, an unregulated banking system could function without deposit insurance and be kept sound purely through market discipline. But probably no country today has fully unregulated banking—although New Zealand and South Africa come close—because even a country prepared to tolerate an occasional bank failure is bound to intervene to avoid a systemic collapse. Indeed, over the past fifty years, most countries, even those without implicit or explicit insurance mechanisms, have rescued depositors when they were faced with widespread bank failures. Implicit insurance tends to be the worst of all possible remedies, because the absence of a well-designed system of deposit protection creates depositor uncertainty, which can aggravate runs on banks, requires in the end greater coverage than otherwise would have been offered, and sticks the government with the bill. To avoid this, countries are moving toward a consensus favoring a system of limited, explicit protection.

The question of *incentives* is crucial in this debate. An organized yet restrained system must provide the right incentives for all parties—small and large depositors, borrowers, bank managers, economic policymakers, and political leaders—while avoiding incentives for these parties to behave in ways that could damage banking and the economy as a whole.

Discipline

The possibility of deposit insurance can tempt involved parties to imagine a wish list of what they might get from this protection—ranging from the obvious (guarding small depositors' money) to the grandiose (attempting to ensure financial stability when the banking system is fundamentally nonviable). Meeting all these divergent interests would lead to an unworkable system, but an insurance system with carefully targeted incentives can encourage interested parties to behave rationally and can contribute to a country's overall economic health.

What would such protection look like? It would first include incentives to reinforce *discipline* in the banking system. It would refrain from interfering with effective bank management, market incentives for large depositors to seek sound banks, and formal regulations to safeguard the banking system. If attention to market forces is balanced and if excessive controls on the market are avoided, a system of deposit insurance can enhance the efficiency of a country's financial markets.

If a deposit insurance system is to offer discipline-encouraging, market-friendly incentives, it must be (1) explicitly formulated in law, (2) compulsory, and (3) accompanied by well-crafted procedures for accounting, loan valuation, regulation, and supervision. It must also (4) have the authority and necessary information to reform faltering banks and deal effectively with insolvent banks. Further, it should (5) be established only after unsound banks have been restructured, (6) treat large, small, private and state-owned banks equally, (7) feature limited coverage of all types of deposits, and (8) provide for prompt reimbursement when a bank fails.

Incentives

The basic goal of a balanced system of deposit insurance is to create the right incentives for self-discipline in the banking system and to avoid incentives that relax discipline. Let us now look at the incentives for each of the main parties: small depositors, large depositors, borrowers, bank managers, economic policymakers, and political leaders. Then, once an outline of an effective system is clear, we will consider the logical steps in setting up and administering such a system.

Small Depositors

The knowledge that their savings are protected gives small depositors confidence in the banking system as a whole. If one bank has a problem, the deposit insurance scheme will reassure depositors in other banks that there is no need to panic. Most countries do indeed insure small depositors—with limits ranging from negligible sums in some countries to $100,000 in the United States and even higher in Italy. A reasonably high limit gives an incentive for individual and small-business depositors to save and protects the retail payments system. And the pressure is off small depositors to try to keep track of their bank's health—which of course would be hard for them.

Large Depositors

Unlike small depositors, large depositors have the resources to monitor the condition of their banks and thus—if there is to be market discipline—do not need unlimited protection for their funds. To avoid interfering with the working of the financial market, large depositors should not be encouraged to count on the insurance system to bail them out if they fail to pay attention to the soundness of their deposits. Therefore, the amount that can be insured needs a cap and conditions should be set out that will in effect limit coverage for large depositors. The system should state whether the cap will apply to each and every deposit at a failed bank, to the sum of all of a depositor's separate accounts at a failed bank, or to the sum of all accounts owned by an individual depositor at all banks that fail during a given period. The system also needs to determine whether it will protect deposits in foreign currencies. The size of the cap will influence the extent of demands placed on the system. A small cap will protect most individuals, but not corporations with access to information on a bank's condition.

This cap will avoid giving large depositors the wrong impression—that they can afford to ignore their bank's soundness. If large depositors pay too little attention to the condition of a problem bank, they may well be complacent about leaving their money in the bank, which in itself provides no incentive for the bank's managers to fix the problem. A workable system of protection needs to make clear the monetary ceiling and needs to warn depositors that it will deal firmly with a failed bank by imposing losses on its owners and its uninsured depositors. An insurance system that can avoid the high cost of bailing out large depositors also serves as the ultimate sign that an effective system of protecting deposits *must* be in tune with market discipline.

Borrowers

Also in keeping with the market are incentives for banks to discipline borrowers. Banks are often the only source of money for those borrowers who lack access to the stock and bond markets. Ill-designed deposit insurance may lull borrowers into a false sense of security or even tempt them to take advantage of the system. Relying on insurance, borrowers may become careless in their personal or business practices or deliberately exploit the protection at the expense of the insurance fund and the taxpayers who pay for it. To prevent this, the system needs to ensure that loans are classified accurately, adequate provisions are made for loan losses, and banks are strongly capitalized.

Bank Managers and Owners

Owners and managers must not be given incentives to engage in behavior detrimental to the whole banking system. Bank managers and owners must either run their banks efficiently or face failure. Deposit insurance is meant to protect the banking system, not poorly run banks. The fact is that bank failures are often self-inflicted by owners and managers who mismanage. Such losses can be reduced if the supervisor closes the bank before it fails totally, since delaying a bank closing or sale tends to increase losses—and to spread them to the banking system as a whole.

Even without deposit insurance, bank managers may pursue their own interests at the expense of the bank. But the problem gets worse with insurance. Managers may indulge in such excesses as high salaries, expensive buildings, and lavish furnishings. To combat this problem, managers could receive an "incentive-compatible contract" to align their interests with those of the owners. When the bank is sound, managers can best protect their professional reputations by keeping it so. However, if a bank begins to fail and no proper incentive exists to protect its capital, managers may join owners in being prepared to "gamble for recovery" by making high-risk loans or to loot or defraud the bank. At that point deposit insurance could increase their opportunities to do so.

Economic Policymakers

The economic policymakers who devise the regulations for banks and who have primary responsibility for creating a deposit insurance system may be led by their own interests to create the wrong incentives. For example, for political reasons, they may favor a system of protection designed to avoid a recession, although banks typically fail only after a recession has started. Regulators may become confused about whom they represent. In banking, serving the public interest involves balancing the sometimes conflicting interests of owners and managers, depositors, other creditors, the insurance fund, and taxpayers. Moreover, regulators may even see themselves as guardians of the banking industry and the institutions it lends to, and they may have the incentive to underprice deposit insurance to subsidize a key industry, such as housing, that depends on bank financing.

Regulators may seek to ingratiate themselves with leaders of the banking industry because it offers them the best chances to get good jobs if they move on from regulation. They believe that their reputations with bankers will be enhanced by presiding over a tranquil financial system and that their careers will be destroyed if they reveal problems for which they might be held responsible. Supervisors therefore have an incentive to keep problems secret in the hope that they can resolve them or leave office gracefully before they deteriorate further and become public knowledge. Deposit protection, if it delays runs on banks, lures supervisors of regulatory agencies into another pitfall: giving more time to failing banks—in their own interest, not the economy's.

Political Leaders

Political leaders are often tempted to procrastinate in taking action on failing banks. The taxpaying citizens to whom they are accountable may not at first perceive the damage being done to them and to healthy economic institutions by delayed supervisory action. The adverse consequence of delay is an increase in the number of failures and the cost of resolving them. Especially when a system of deposit insurance is in place, problems can be postponed if they are inconspicuous because taxpayers are a diffuse group and may not lobby effectively. At the same time, regulators may fear that disciplinary action will immediately result in a public expression of outrage from those being disciplined, who will complain that the supervisory actions are premature and punitive. To force regulators and supervisors to act in the public interest, political leaders need to legislate to limit their discretion, to require them to act in appropriate circumstances, and to reveal the fiscal implication of their actions. (This was the objective of the 1991 U.S. Federal Deposit Insurance Corporation Improvement Act.) In short, regulators should have a strong incentive to close or sell problem banks right away.

The unfortunate reality is that politicians are commonly targeted by bankers, who form a successful pressure group with powerful political connections in most countries. Politicians may intercede to win forbearance for bankers who do business in their constituency or have contributed to campaign funds. Insurance-induced creditor inertia over the conditions and activities of a bank enables politicians to practice special-interest politics by interfering in the discipline process and by encouraging supervisors to temporize before the inevitable bailout of the failing bank. This problem occurs in many countries, but can be countered by reforming the system of campaign finance, carefully crafting laws that limit regulatory discretion, mandating prompt corrective action and closure, releasing information on the condition of banks, and encouraging the independence of the supervisory and insurance agencies and the central bank.

An Effective System

Given the various incentives for parties interested in the banking system, how can protection be successfully implemented? Overall, the right incentives suggest a system of deposit insurance that would minimize the number of bank failures, resolve those that occur rapidly with a minimum of uncertainty and expense to banks or the government, and not interfere with the financial market or the overall economy. Let us envision some basic steps toward such a system.

Step One: Create the Basis

The first step is to create the political and legislative basis for a legally mandated, formally structured insurance system. This explicit system will empower the authorities to avoid the wrong incentives and implement the right ones. (Implicit systems—based on the authorities' public statements or past actions in protecting state-owned banks, guaranteeing their loans, and intervening elsewhere to protect depositors—are notoriously ineffective.) The lessons of history will be useful for policymakers seeking to establish a basis for strong, ongoing structures to protect deposits.

Step Two: Consider the Structure of Banking

The second step toward a successful system is to examine the efficiency and equity of any proposed insurance scheme. Economists and policymakers need to consider cooperatively exactly how banks can function best under insurance. For example, in a banking crisis, while macroeconomic concerns might suggest that small banks be promptly liquidated while large banks be given forbearance and ultimately bailed out, this favorable treatment of large banks may be understandable but does not represent equal treatment for all.

Another structural issue that needs considering is bank ownership. Private banks and state-owned banks operating in the same system may again result in unequal treatment. Private banks may be allowed to fail, while state banks that have been weakened as a result of lending for political rather than commercial purposes may be granted forbearance and bailed out. In addition, private banks may be forced to pay (through higher insurance premiums) for the political preference that the state banks receive.

Ownership of banks by industrial firms or financial groups can be a structural problem if the banks are treated by their owners as captive financiers. Deposit insurance may then provide an opportunity for owners to abuse their banks so they can subsidize other interests. While regulations on lending to related parties and to single borrowers may be established to prevent such abuse, these regulations can be notoriously difficult to administer. In these circumstances, deposit insurance can actually help an unscrupulous owner to rob his own bank.

Step Three: Build an Administrative Framework

Once the basic structural issues of banking are resolved, the third step is to consider the actual condition of the banking system and then to build an appropriate administrative framework. Before a system starts up, policymakers need to examine the capital condition and the loan portfolios of the banking system as a whole as well as the capital available to each bank and the condition of its individual loan portfolio before allowing it to join the system. If the capital base of individual banks is inadequate, it would be wise to recapitalize them before they join the system. Further, there is a need for a framework of workable regulations, accounting procedures, loan valuations, audits, reporting rules, and supervision. Finally, publishing nonproprietary information will help bank customers protect their own interests and will help impose market discipline on the banking system.

Step Four: Ensure Independence

The fourth step is to make sure that the government insuring agency is put on a firm legal foundation with the independent responsibility to resolve bank failures. It should invest its resources conservatively and have the power to borrow if necessary in anticipation of future revenue. If a country has a privately administered system, as 11 countries do, it may be necessary for some public agency to close failed banks. It is essential that the legal basis for deposit protection be strong and definite regarding property rights, closing failed banks, and the independence of the supervisory agency from the central bank. The agency should be free from political interference. The central bank, supervisory agency, and insuring agency should have enough coordinated authority that they can act decisively to publish and enforce regulations and to take quick corrective action and to close failed banks promptly.

Step Five: Provide Funding

The fifth step is to provide sufficient funding and skilled staff to launch the system. These initial resources can be obtained in several ways: (1) place a start-up levy solely on the banks; (2) share the levy among the commercial banks, the central bank, and the treasury; (3) hold the government alone responsible for meeting the agency's initial financial needs; or (4) start the system without accumulated funds but grant authority for the agency to borrow to meet its needs.

A decision also has to be made whether official funding will be permanent or is to be repaid by the banks over time. If a system starts up with funds that the public perceives to be insufficient, it will not win their confidence and risks insolvency. Insolvent systems are prone to forbearance, costly forms of resolution, and crises (as was the U.S. Federal Savings and Loan Insurance Corporation in the 1980s).

The insurance agency's staff may at first be borrowed from the central bank, which is likely to have a pool of employees with the right experience. Later, the insuring agency can train its own staff, which should mature with experience.

Step Six: Standardize Operations

The sixth step is to devise methods to run the system during normal times. The tested techniques of the insurance industry suggest that the system underwrite, control, and transfer part of its risk exposure. It can take several steps to underwrite its risk by matching its resources to the demands expected to be placed upon them. It does this by choosing the risks and risk-takers it is willing to insure, denying coverage to others, obtaining and disseminating information to distinguish good risks and bad risks, pricing the insured risks carefully, setting premiums sufficient to build a fund that will be adequate in most situations, and obtaining backup resources for periods of extended crisis. There are many technical concerns regarding this step that are beyond the scope of this paper. But let us look at one question: how banks qualify for deposit insurance coverage.

Although standard life and property insurance firms can deny coverage initially or refuse to renew it for customers that do not meet the criteria they impose, a deposit insurer has less leeway. While it is feasible to decline to charter a bank that does not meet the deposit insurance criteria, it is more difficult to deny protection once a bank is already in business because this would, in effect, mean withdrawing the bank's license. Restrictions on licensing therefore become crucial to selecting the risks the insurer will take. Demanding conditions should be met before a bank is granted any license that is accompanied by a right to deposit protection. While many countries grant licenses in perpetuity, others require periodic re-licensing to enhance control over the quality of banks already in operation.

Step Seven: Plan for a Banking Crisis

The seventh step is to make a careful plan for facing a crisis in the banking system. Here is where deposit insurance parts company with other kinds of insurance. A normal insured risk covers the possibility of a claim resulting from a rare and isolated incident. The opposite is true of a banking crisis, during which failures are frequent and connected. If the government has an adequate tax base, its help can avoid a meltdown of the financial system. A mechanism needs to be in place to supplement the funds of the deposit protection system.

The Search for Financial Stability

Policymakers and political leaders contemplating taking these seven steps toward a feasible system of deposit insurance should keep in mind the need to strengthen and create *incentives* for balanced *discipline.* The system needs to reinforce, not interfere with, incentives for bank managers to use discipline, because sound management of banks is the main guardian of a stable financial system. The system thus needs to provide incentives for the right market discipline and regulatory decisions to support strong bank managers. Regulation must be restrained so it does not stifle innovation and economic growth. Thus a deposit insurance system, created in accord with both market and regulatory discipline, that reinforces managers' efforts will help the banking system to work efficiently.

The Economic Issues Series

1. *Growth in East Asia: What We Can and What We Cannot Infer.* Michael Sarel. 1996.

2. *Does the Exchange Rate Regime Matter for Inflation and Growth?* Atish R. Ghosh, Anne-Marie Gulde, Jonathan D. Ostry, and Holger Wolf. 1996.

3. *Confronting Budget Deficits.* 1996.

4. *Fiscal Reforms That Work.* C. John McDermott and Robert F. Wescott. 1996.

5. *Transformations to Open Market Operations: Developing Economies and Emerging Markets.* Stephen H. Axilrod. 1996.

6. *Why Worry About Corruption?* Paolo Mauro. 1997.

7. *Sterilizing Capital Inflows.* Jang-Yung Lee. 1997.

8. *Why Is China Growing So Fast?* Zuliu Hu and Mohsin S. Khan. 1997.

9. *Protecting Bank Deposits.* Gillian Garcia. 1997.